MOTORCYCLE RACING

written and photographed by Ed Radlauer

622 RODIER DRIVE • GLENDALE, CALIFORNIA 91201

Copyright © 1970 by Bowmar Publishing Corp.
All rights reserved. No part of this book may be reproduced
in any form without permission from the publishers. Printed
in the United States of America.
International Standard Book Number: hardcover 0-8372-0699-5 softcover 0-8372-0695-2
Library of Congress catalog card number 73-737271

First Printing	November 1970
Second Printing	April 1971
Third Printing	July 1971
Fourth Printing	September 1972

What kind of motorcycle racing do *you* like? Is it motorcycle Drag Racing? In motorcycle Drag Racing you need a machine with power to *accelerate* to a high speed. You have to accelerate to get to the finish line ahead of the other rider.

Before you can race with another rider you have to *qualify*. When it's time to qualify you bring your bike up to the lights at the starting line and watch the *Christmas tree*. When the light on the Christmas tree turns green, you go! You may go as fast as 170 miles per hour!

The drag strip is a straight, flat, quarter mile track. For straight, flat racing a cycle should have a long or extended *frame* and *front fork rake*. An extended front fork rake helps the rider keep the front wheel on the ground. It also helps keep the bike moving straight.

In a drag race you qualify by making a run over the quarter mile. *Timing lights* tell your speed and E.T. or *elapsed time* for the run. A ten second E.T. means it took ten seconds to cover the quarter mile. That's a good E.T. for a bike!

The timing lights on the drag strip work when a wheel cuts through a beam of light. Some riders put a piece of metal or plastic in the front wheel of their bikes. The metal or plastic in the wheel helps the timing lights work by cutting through the beam of light.

You may like a two engine machine for Drag Racing. Two engines give twice the power. However, because of the extra weight, they *do not* give twice the speed. But even with the extra weight, when both engines work right and run together, you move!

A short handlebar is good in Drag Racing. It lets the rider lie flat and hold his arms close to his body. With your body low and arms close together steering and balancing are easier on a straight track.

It takes more than good riding to win at Drag Racing. Hard work by the pit crew is part of the job. You can't win a race on a bike that won't run. That's why everyone on the pit crew has a job. And he better do it!

The safety rules say you must wear *leathers* and a *helmet* to be in a drag race. The rules also say that you must put your feet on the *pegs* as soon as you leave the starting line. With leathers, helmet, and feet on the pegs a rider is pretty safe.

After you qualify, you go into a class according to engine size and E.T. *Elimination* races are run according to classes.

In an elimination race, the loser is eliminated. He is out of the day's racing. The winner of an elimination race goes into the next round of races and hopes to run in the last race, the *final* elimination.

There's plenty of straight track in a *Gran Prix* race. But there's much more. There are three miles of curves and sharp turns. For this kind of racing, you need a machine that is fast, has good brakes, and is easy to steer.

On the *straightaway* riders get up plenty of speed, as much as 135 miles per hour in some of the heavy classes. At 135 miles per hour there's plenty of wind, too. Is that why the rider is down behind the *fairing*?

When a Gran Prix motorcycle goes off the straight-away and into a curve it needs good brakes. Without good brakes you might change the curve into a straight-away. Then you'd be breaking the rules. You might break a few other things, too.

With good steering control and balance, you can get through a long curve without slowing. The *rake* or angle of the *front fork* is important for steering. Long rakes like those on drag bikes won't steer much at all. Short rakes turn you so fast you can find yourself going sideways.

Are these riders out looking for something they lost? No, they're hoping they don't lose their balance, because that's what it takes to handle a Gran Prix *sidehack* motorcycle. Sidehack is the only two-man motorcycle racing there is, and it takes two-man balance.

If sidehack riders don't balance the cycle, they either have to slow down or tip over. They must remember to lean toward the inside of curves. If they don't remember to lean toward the inside of curves, they'll land upside down on the outside of the curve. Then they lose.

As in all racing, Gran Prix rules say cycles must pass *inspection* before the races. Inspectors with sharp eyes look over the tires, frame, brakes, and engine. If the bike passes inspection, the inspector puts the cycle in a racing class according to engine size.

In some Gran Prix races, the riders *push start* their machines. To push start a machine each rider holds the clutch in, pushes his cycle, jumps on, lets the clutch out, and hopes the engine will *fire*. If an engine doesn't fire, the rider gets to watch the race from behind the fence.

Riders try to get to the front of the pack as soon as the race is on. Sometimes the turns get crowded, but a crowd is OK as long as everyone is headed the same way. And it's fun to race in a pack because it takes good handling.

But even if you're not in a pack, Gran Prix racing is fun. There's the long smooth track, your machine, and the wind singing around the fairing.

And, if you don't have a fairing to keep the wind off, let it sing through your helmet.

If flat, smooth Gran Prix or drag tracks aren't what you like, you'll probably want to try *Moto Cross* racing. The track for Moto Cross has steep trails, sand pits, jumps, hills, some straightaway, and sometimes even a water crossing.

For the steep, rough hills in the Moto Cross track, riders need powerful, lightweight machines. Since most lightweight machines use *two cycle* engines, that is almost all you see in a Moto Cross race. A two cycle engine gives quick *acceleration* when you need it.

And you really need acceleration at the start of a race. Every rider wants to be out of the pack and over the first hill. With power, control, and good *knobby* tires you have a chance to stay out front.

But to climb hills you need more than knobby tires. You need good handling, power and control, too. If you lose control you may dump your bike. Just think, there may be thirty more riders coming along. And they are not about to slow, stop, or dump *their* bikes!

You'd better not go in a Moto Cross race if you like to keep your feet dry. Many Moto Cross tracks have a water crossing. The crossing isn't deep, but the water in the crossing is just as wet as any other water.

Wet feet in a Moto Cross race isn't such bad news. But wet *ignition is*. With wet ignition your engine quits because there is no *spark*. No spark, means no engine. *You* quit the race.

You can tell this rider doesn't have wet ignition. He's found the right way to take the jumps on the Moto Cross track. Pull your machine up, lean back, and put the rear wheel down first. If you don't lean back and put the rear wheel down first you may spend part of the race sitting on the ground.

Sometimes the track is very narrow. If it's too narrow to pass you could try to go over the rider in front of you. But don't. On any track it's against the rules, a way to be disqualified.

Moto Cross racing, like all motorcycle racing, takes control, balance, and good handling. Riders who have good machines and know how to handle them come out winners, even if they're not in first place.

If you don't like Drag Racing, Gran Prix, or Moto Cross racing, you may want to try a *tricycle*.

With a three wheel tricycle and a big eight cylinder engine, you don't have to worry about balance, control or handling — much! And with an eight cylinder engine you'll be sure to hear the wind sing through your helmet.